Starving

the

Anger

Gremlin

FOR CHILDREN AGED 5–9

by the same author

Starving the Anxiety Gremlin for Children Aged 5–9
A Cognitive Behavioural Therapy Workbook
on Anxiety Management
ISBN 978 1 84905 492 8
eISBN 978 0 85700 902 9

Starving the Anger Gremlin
A Cognitive Behavioural Therapy Workbook
on Anger Management for Young People
ISBN 978 1 84905 286 3
eISBN 978 0 85700 621 9

Starving the Anxiety Gremlin
A Cognitive Behavioural Therapy Workbook
on Anxiety Management for Young People
ISBN 978 1 84905 341 9
eISBN 978 0 85700 673 8

Starving the Stress Gremlin
A Cognitive Behavioural Therapy Workbook
on Stress Management for Young People
ISBN 978 1 84905 340 2
eISBN 978 0 85700 672 1

Banish Your Body Image Thief
A Cognitive Behavioural Therapy Workbook on Building
Positive Body Image for Young People
ISBN 978 1 84905 463 8
eISBN 978 0 85700 842 8

Banish Your Self-Esteem Thief
A Cognitive Behavioural Therapy Workbook on Building
Positive Self-Esteem for Young People
ISBN 978 1 84905 462 1
eISBN 978 0 85700 841 1

of related interest

The Red Beast
Controlling Anger in Children with Asperger's Syndrome
K.I. Al-Ghani
Illustrated by Haitham Al-Ghani
ISBN 978 1 84310 943 3
eISBN 978 1 84642 848 7

Anger Management Games for Children
Deborah M. Plummer
Illustrated by Jane Serrurier
ISBN 978 1 84310 628 9
eISBN 978 1 84642 775 6

Starving
the
Anger
Gremlin

FOR CHILDREN AGED 5–9

A COGNITIVE BEHAVIOURAL THERAPY WORKBOOK ON ANGER MANAGEMENT

KATE COLLINS-DONNELLY

Jessica Kingsley *Publishers*
London and Philadelphia

First published in 2014
by Jessica Kingsley Publishers
73 Collier Street
London N1 9BE, UK
and
400 Market Street, Suite 400
Philadelphia, PA 19106, USA

www.jkp.com

Library of Congress Cataloging in Publication Data
Collins-Donnelly, Kate.
  Starving the anger gremlin for children aged 5-9 : a cognitive behavioural
therapy workbook on anger management / Kate Collins-Donnelly.
     pages cm
  Includes bibliographical references.
  ISBN 978-1-84905-493-5 (alk. paper)
  1. Anger. 2. Anger in children. 3. Cognitive therapy for children. I. Title.
  BF575.A5.C653 2014
  155.4'1247--dc23
                          2014005347

British Library Cataloguing in Publication Data
A CIP catalogue record for this book is available from the British Library

ISBN 978 1 84905 493 5
eISBN 978 0 85700 885 5

Printed and bound by Bell and Bain Ltd, Glasgow

Contents

Acknowledgements

First, I would like to thank all the children, parents, practitioners and colleagues who have inspired me to develop this workbook. I would also like to thank everyone whom I have worked with at Jessica Kingsley Publishers, especially my editor Caroline, for their invaluable help with all my books to date. It is always a joy to work with you. Thank you also to Tina Gothard for her fantastic Anger Gremlin illustrations used throughout this workbook. Tina, it was a pleasure to work with you. And last, but by no means least, a huge thank you goes to Maria for her motivation, inspiration, support and guidance.

About the Author

Hi! I'm Kate, and I have worked for several years providing support for children, young people and their parents on the emotional issues that children and young people face today, including anger. I have also provided training and guidance for professionals from a variety of disciplines on how to support children, young people and their families when a child or young person is suffering with issues such as anger. Through this work, it became evident that there was a need for a book aimed directly at children aged 5 to 9 years on how to control their anger, and as a result, *Starving the Anger Gremlin for Children Aged 5–9* was born.

This book contains stories, puzzles and activities to help you learn about what anger is, why we get angry, how we think, feel and act when we get angry and the effects that anger can have. It also provides a step-by-step guide to controlling your anger by starving your Anger Gremlin!

I hope you find this workbook fun as well as packed with useful ways to get your anger under control once and for all!

Happy reading and good luck with starving your Anger Gremlin!

Kate

1

Why Read This Book?

This book is here to help you if...

You often feel angry

You hit, punch or kick people or things when you get angry

You say nasty things to people when you get angry

You shout or scream at people when you get angry

You bottle up your anger

You break, bang or throw things when you get angry

You hurt yourself when you get angry

By reading this book you will learn about your anger. You will also meet a creature called the Anger Gremlin. The Anger Gremlin's favourite food is your anger. He wants you to feed him lots and lots of anger so he can get bigger and bigger. But this workbook will teach you how to starve him of his favourite food so you will...

Get angry less often

Act in calmer ways when you do get angry

So starving your Anger Gremlin is your mission! And you will learn how to do this through fun puzzles, activities and stories! The answers to these puzzles and activities are at the back of the book. Plus, don't forget you can get an adult to help you along the way if you get stuck with any of them. You'll also get to draw lots of things too! And you can colour in any of the pictures you see throughout this workbook. In fact, why not colour in the pictures on the pages that you have just read!

Happy colouring!

I have one more thing to tell you about this book, which is that every time you complete a chapter you will earn two...

rewards!

Let's take a look at what these rewards are!

Reward 1:
The Starving the Anger Gremlin Star!

At the end of each chapter, you will collect a star. You can have fun colouring the stars in using whatever colours and funky patterns you like! When you have collected all 11 stars, you will have successfully completed this workbook and you will know exactly how to achieve your mission to starve your Anger Gremlin!

Why not colour this one in as a practice?

Reward 2:
The Just for Fun Puzzles!

You will also have two **Just for Fun Puzzles** to choose
from at the end of each chapter as a reward for
all your hard work along the way. And if you like
you can even complete both puzzles!

Here's a **Just for Fun Puzzle** for you to try out now!

Escape the Anger Gremlin!

Quick! Quick! Escape from the Anger Gremlin by finding your way through the maze. Be careful as there are two routes out, but one will take you longer than the other!

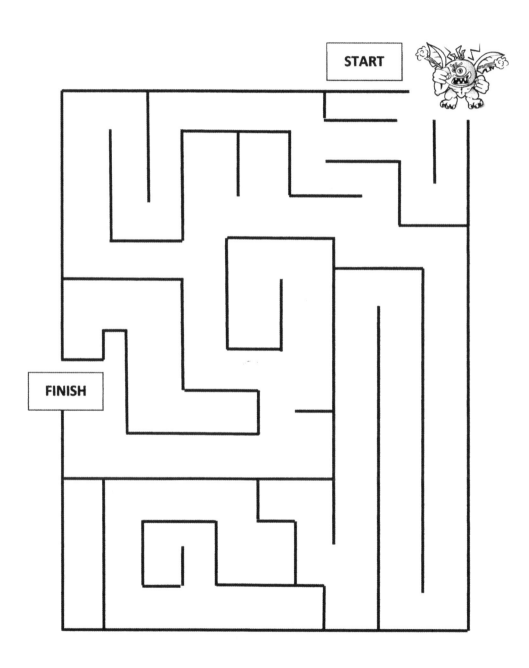

2

Let's Meet a Mystery Creature!

We're All Going on a Jungle Holiday!

You are an adventurous explorer trekking through the heart of the African jungle.

Along the way you pass lions, giraffes, monkeys, hippos, rhinos, elephants, zebras, snakes and birds of many colours. You stop to marvel at these amazing animals, but these are not the mystery creature that you are looking for.

Over the page is a jungle path. As you trek along this path, you will find a number of clues to the name of the mystery creature that you seek. Follow the clues and see if you can work out who they are describing. And keep your eyes peeled as you might spot the mystery creature hidden amongst the other animals! Draw the mystery creature or write down his name in the magnifying glass at the end of the jungle trail. Also why not colour in the animals that you pass as you move from clue to clue?

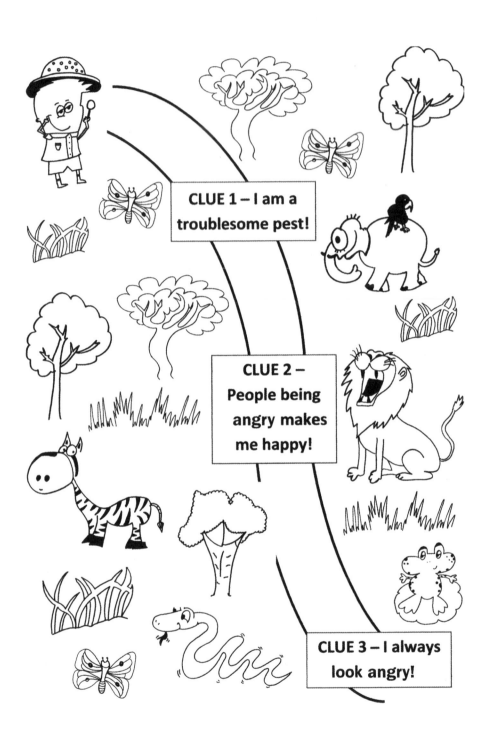

CLUE 1 – I am a troublesome pest!

CLUE 2 – People being angry makes me happy!

CLUE 3 – I always look angry!

CLUE 5 – The more anger you feed me, the bigger and bigger I get!

CLUE 4 – My favourite food is your anger!

Here's the creature you were looking for and his name is...

the Anger Gremlin!

Step 1 in starving the Anger Gremlin is learning who he is. You will learn more about the Anger Gremlin as you work through this book. But for now, why not colour him in? You can make his colours match those on the front of this book or you can choose your own – the choice is yours!

Because you have been such an amazing jungle explorer and completed Step 1 of your mission to starve your Anger Gremlin, you have earned your first **Starving the Anger Gremlin Star**! Be proud and colour in your star!

Now have a go at one or both of these **Just for Fun Puzzles** as another reward for your great work so far! Enjoy!

Gremlins Galore!

The triangle below is full of Anger Gremlins and stars. How many Anger Gremlins are there? Write the answer on the line below.

There are _____ Anger Gremlins in the triangle.

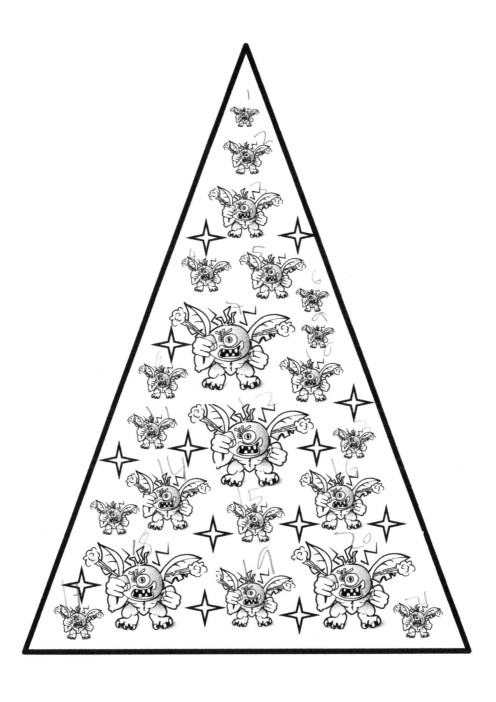

Word Multiplication!

See how many words you can make out of the letters that are used to spell...

the Anger Gremlin.

Write your answers in the box below. I've found two for you to start you off!

Germ

Green

3

Let's Learn about Feelings!

Learning about feelings is Step 2 in your mission to starve your Anger Gremlin!

Feelings, Feelings and More Feelings!

It is normal for everyone to have lots of different feelings every day, such as feeling excited about a school trip or feeling happy when you win a board game! Another word for feelings is...

emotions.

Complete the two activities below to learn about some different types of feelings.

Feelings or Not Feelings? You Decide!

Below is a picture of a girl. Your first task is to colour her in. So have fun colouring!

While you were colouring in the girl, did you notice that there are lots of words written all around her? Some of them are feelings and some aren't. Your next task is to colour in those that are feelings. Good luck!

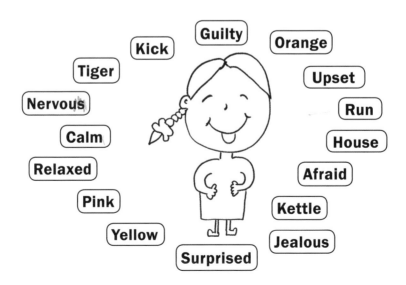

Find the Feelings!

See if you can find the following six feelings in the word search below. Circle or highlight the feelings when you find them. I've found one for you to get you started!

HAPPY   SAD   WORRIED   EXCITED   SCARED   PROUD

W	T	S	A	D	E	H
O	K	C	B	M	X	A
R	V	A	Z	H	C	P
R	O	R	N	I	I	P
I	R	E	G	K	T	Y
E	J	D	Y	E	E	O
D	P	R	O	U	D	B

Well done! You've now learnt the names of some feelings. Next let's think about how people's faces look when they have certain feelings by doing the activity below.

The Face and Feeling Mix-Up!

Below you will find six faces and each one shows a different feeling. Each face also has a label under it with the name of a feeling. However, the naughty Anger Gremlin has mixed up the labels on all the faces!

See if you can work out which face should go with which label. Draw lines to match up the correct faces and feelings. Again, I've done one for you to start you off! Why not colour in the faces too for an extra bit of fun?

Worried   **Sad**

Excited   **Proud**

Scared   **Happy**

All Feelings Are Different

- You might have some feelings **regularly** but other feelings only **occasionally**.
- Some feelings will hang around for **a long time** but others will **come and go quickly**.
- Some feelings will be **really strong** and others will be **less strong**.

All of this is normal!

Why Do We Have Feelings?

When we have feelings, we usually have them in response to certain situations, events, places, people or objects. Below are six boxes. Each box contains a feeling. I would like you to draw a picture in each box of what makes you happy, sad, worried, excited, scared and proud.

I feel happy when...

I feel sad when...

I feel worried when...

I feel excited when...

I feel scared when...

I feel proud when...

Wow! You've completed Step 2 in starving your Anger Gremlin. Well done! Give yourself a big clap, feel proud and colour in your second **Starving the Anger Gremlin Star**!

Now try completing one or both of the following **Just for Fun Puzzles** as a reward for your brilliant work so far! Have fun!

Give the Anger Gremlin a Makeover!

Colour in the Anger Gremlin using the colour code below:

1 = Blue   **2 = Red**   **3 = Green**   **4 = Orange**

Then for any parts of the Anger Gremlin that don't contain a number, pick your own colours. Use your imagination! Happy colouring!

'What Am I?' Riddle

The answer to each line of the following riddle is a letter of the alphabet. When you add all these letters together in order you will spell a word. See if you can work out the word. I have given you the answer to the first and last lines of the riddle to show you how it's done. Happy solving!

My first is in FURY but never in PROUDLY **F**

My second is in RELAXED and also in UPSET ☐

My third is in BRAVE and also in CHILLED ☐

My fourth is in LOVE but never in ENVIOUS ☐

My fifth is in AFRAID but never in FEARED ☐

My sixth is in TENSE and also in DOWN ☐

My seventh is in GIDDY and also in GLUM ☐

My eighth is in NERVOUS and also in SAD **S**

WHAT AM I?

THE ANSWER IS F _ _ _ _ _ _ S

4

What Is Anger?

Step 3 in your mission to starve your Anger Gremlin is to learn what anger is.

Anger Is a Feeling Too!

Anger is another type of feeling or emotion that we can all experience sometimes. Draw an angry-looking face in the box below.

Draw an angry face

Different Words for Angry

There are lots of different words that mean angry. The letters in the boxes below spell out four words meaning angry in a spiral shape. Can you spot them all? Colour in each word in a different colour.

HINT: Start with the letter 'M'.

S	N	N	O	Y
U	A	A	D	E
O	S	M	C	D
I	S	O	R	F
R				U

Everybody Feels Angry at Times!

Now you know that anger is a feeling and that there are lots of other words that mean the same thing, it's also important to know that we all feel angry at times. I'm sure if you ask your mum or dad, your brothers and sisters or your friends, they will all tell you they have felt angry at some point in their lives.

Here's a story about an eight-year-old boy called Martin who felt angry one day at school. You can colour in the pictures as you read the story if you like.

Martin the Magician Gets Mad!

It was the day of the talent contest at Paxton Primary School and Martin was buzzing with excitement. He had been practising his magic tricks for weeks and couldn't wait to perform them in front of the children and parents who were gathered in the school hall.

The contest started and Martin watched other children act, sing, tell jokes, dance and juggle.

Suddenly a teacher called Mrs Hopkins shouted, 'Martin Simpson, it's your turn!'

Martin's heart began to pound nervously in his chest. But he took a deep breath, stood up and walked confidently to the stage.

'Let the magic begin!' said Mrs Hopkins before leaving Martin alone on the stage.

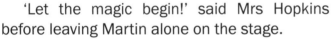

Martin did card tricks and made objects disappear and reappear. Children in the audience gasped and cheered. Martin couldn't stop smiling when he had finished as he'd had so much fun.

At the end of the contest, Mrs Hopkins began to announce the prize winners. 'Third prize goes to Sally Smith!'

Sally Smith ran up to the stage with her lucky tap shoes still on her feet. Martin clapped. 'Sally's dance was good', he thought.

'Second prize goes to Felix Jones!'

'Blimey,' thought Martin. 'I thought Felix would have won. His singing was awesome.'

'Finally, first prize goes to Martin Simpson!'

Martin could hardly believe it. People shouted congratulations to him as he walked up to the stage in a daze.

'Did I really win?' asked Martin as Mrs Hopkins handed him his trophy. Mrs Hopkins laughed and nodded. Martin didn't need to be told to smile when the school photographer took his picture alongside Felix and Sally; he couldn't stop beaming from ear to ear anyway!

After the photograph was taken, Martin stepped down from the stage and went to find his mum in the audience. On the way, he bumped into George, an older child who had taken part in the contest but not won a prize.

Martin smiled at George and said, 'I thought your juggling was really good. You should have won a prize.'

George scowled. 'Well, I thought your magic tricks were silly and I don't know why you won. I thought you looked like a weirdo.' And before Martin got to reply, George stormed off.

Martin felt himself get really hot. His hands were shaking. His muscles were tense. Martin felt angry!

The End!

There's a question for you to answer about Martin in the box below. You can write or draw your answer in the box or you can tell your answer to whoever is reading this book with you.

Why do you think Martin felt angry?

BECAUSE George Said that
HE Looked LIKe a wierdo

You probably worked out that Martin felt angry about the mean things that George had said to him. It is normal to feel angry, like Martin did, **if someone says or does hurtful things to you**.

It is also normal to feel angry **when something unfair happens**. For example, if your mum blames you for breaking a vase in the kitchen even though it was the cat that did it!

When Is Anger a Problem?

Even though it is normal to feel angry at times, our anger can become a problem if we feel angry a lot and/or show it in ways that aren't good for us or other people. The following puzzle will teach you more about when anger becomes a problem.

Find the Pairs!

There are two sets of boxes on the next pages.

- Set A contains six reasons why children's anger can become a problem.
- Set B contains pictures of some children whose anger has become a problem.

Match up each child's story with the reason why their anger has become a problem. Write down the reason numbers in the correct boxes. I have done one for you to show you how it's done. You can colour in the pictures too if you want to.

SET A

Reason 1: It isn't good for you if you feel angry a lot	Reason 2: It isn't good if you hurt other people when you get angry
Reason 3: It isn't good if you break things when you get angry	Reason 4: It isn't good for you if you bottle your anger up inside
Reason 5: It isn't good for you if you hurt yourself when you get angry	Reason 6: Anger isn't good for you if it has bad results

SET B

Pippa aged eight keeps her anger inside of her until it gets so big that she explodes at someone

Reason Number ___4___

Sammie aged seven gets angry about something every day

Reason Number ___

Karl aged nine hits himself when he gets angry

Reason Number ___5___

Thomas aged six smashes up his
toys when he gets angry

Reason Number ___3___

Jenny aged seven gets into trouble at home for getting angry with her sister

Reason Number _____

Mollie aged five hits her mum when she gets angry

Reason Number _____

Don't worry if any of these stories remind you of you because this book will help you to control your anger problems. And you have learnt lots of things already that will help you to do this. So give yourself a big clap for completing Step 3 in starving your Anger Gremlin and colour in your third **Starving the Anger Gremlin Star**!

Now complete one or both of the following **Just for Fun Puzzles** as a reward for all you've learnt! Enjoy!

Go Dotty!

Join up the dots on the next page to reveal a picture. Start with dot number 1 and finish with dot number 90. Then why not colour in the picture when you have finished?

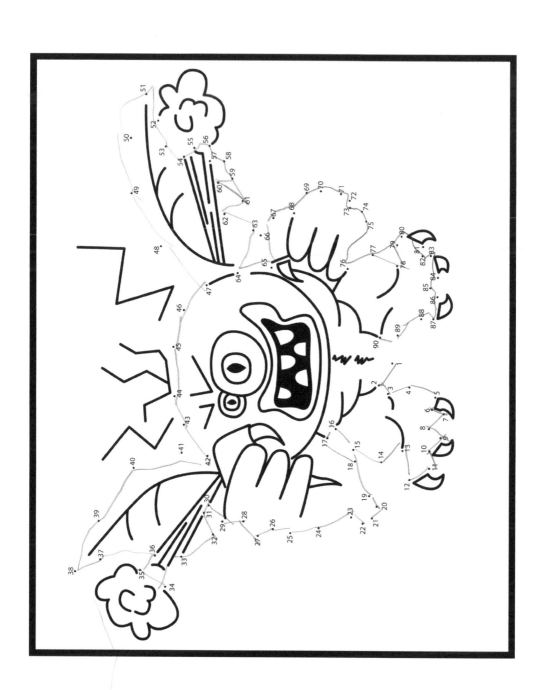

Word Hunt

How many times can you find the word 'anger' in the face below?

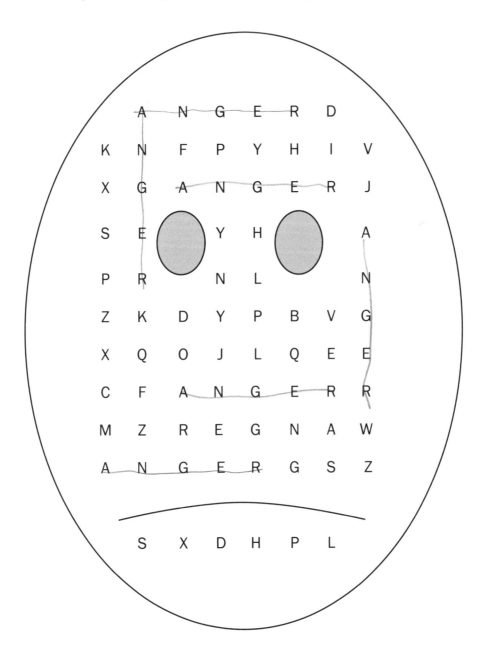

A N G E R D
K N F P Y H I V
X G A N G E R J
S E Y H A
P R N L N
Z K D Y P B V G
X Q O J L Q E E
C F A N G E R R
M Z R E G N A W
A N G E R G S Z
S X D H P L

I can find the word 'anger' _____ times.

5

Things We Get Angry About

Step 4 in your mission to starve your Anger Gremlin is to learn about anger triggers.

Anger Triggers

Like any other feeling, when we feel angry it is in response to something that we call a...

trigger.

Anger triggers can be:

People

For example,
your parents.

Pets

For example, your dog.

Someone's actions

For example, your mum telling you off.

Places

For example, school.

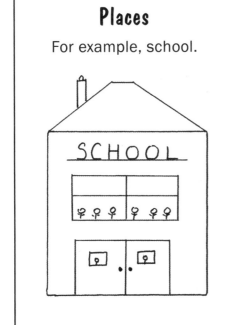

Situations

For example, losing at a computer game.

You are about to read a story about a seven-year-old girl called Amy. Amy gets angry a lot. But she is about to have one of her angriest days ever!

As you read the story you will notice that there are missing words. All these missing words are Amy's anger triggers.

I want you to fill in the missing words using the pictures on the next page. But beware! There is one picture on the page that doesn't fit in the story!

You can photocopy the pictures on the next page and cut them out with an adult's help. Please be very careful. And then you need to glue or tape the right picture in the right place in the story. Or you can draw the pictures in the boxes instead.

Match These Pictures to the Following Story!

Angry Amy's Awfully Angry Day!

Amy woke from a deep sleep when her mum walked into her room and shouted, 'Good morning! It's time to get up as we're going to visit your grandparents today.'

'Ugh! What time is it?' asked a still very sleepy Amy.

'8am,' said Amy's dad as he popped his head around her bedroom door.

Amy started to shout at her...

'You know I hate getting up early! I hate you both too!'

'Don't speak to us like that, Amy!' said her dad. 'Get dressed and then come and help your mum feed all the animals before we go out.'

Amy threw a pillow at her bedroom door as her parents closed it behind them. She got dressed as slowly as she could and then stomped down the stairs.

Amy started to feed her pets but got cross with her...

...for jumping off the kitchen window, knocking over its food bowl and spilling its tinned tuna all over the floor.

Amy then got mad at her...

...for spilling water all over its hutch. Amy even got mad with her...

...for swimming away from the food she put in the tank instead of eating it!

When Amy had finally finished feeding her pets, she joined her parents in the car and travelled to her grandparents' house. Amy loved her grandparents, but they often teased her about silly little things. Today, when her Grandma and Granddad Timpson started to tease her about her new hairstyle, Amy got very hot. Her hands began to shake and her face went red.

'Why do you have to be so mean? I don't like you any more!' Amy screamed at her...

Amy was made to apologise to her grandparents for her outburst and on the way home in the car her parents told her that she was grounded for the rest of the day. This made Amy even angrier!

The End!

Your Anger Triggers

Write down or draw the types of people, pets, places, situations or people's actions that you often get angry about in the box below. If it is easier for you, why not talk to an adult about this or cut pictures out of magazines and comics and make a collage of the things that you get angry about?

The things I get angry about are... when

My mum say bad words

and I say them

back at her

because she

deserves it

Congratulations! You've learnt lots about anger triggers and completed Step 4 in starving your Anger Gremlin. Be proud and colour in your fourth **Starving the Anger Gremlin Star**!

Now complete one or both of the following **Just for Fun Puzzles** as a reward for all your hard work! Enjoy!

How Many Gremlins?

There are lots of Anger Gremlin pictures in this chapter. See how many you can find and write your answer below.

There are _____ Anger Gremlins in this chapter.

Odd Gremlin Out

Look at the pictures below and see if you can work out which Anger Gremlin is the odd gremlin out.

6

Why We Get Angry

Step 5 in your mission to starve your Anger Gremlin is to learn why we get angry.

Everyone Gets Angry about Different Things

By now you will have realised that we don't all get angry about the same things. What one child gets angry about, another child may feel completely different about. Here's a story about two nine-year-old boys to show you what I mean.

Shawn and Ben Get into Trouble!

Shawn and Ben are in the same class at school. Ben works very hard at school but sometimes gets distracted by his best friend Shawn.

It's Friday afternoon and Shawn is bored listening to his teacher, Mrs Phillips, talk about maths. So Shawn starts to pull faces at Ben. Ben giggles quietly but then continues to listen to Mrs Phillips.

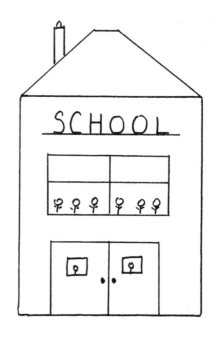

Next Shawn starts to draw silly pictures on a piece of paper he has in front of him. Both boys start laughing a little too loudly!

'Would you like to tell the rest of us what is so funny?' asks Mrs Phillips.

Both boys say nothing so Mrs Phillips walks over to their table and picks up Shawn's piece of paper. Staring at Mrs Phillips is a picture that Shawn has drawn of her.

Mrs Phillips crumples up the piece of paper in her hand and says, 'I will speak to you and your parents after school today.'

'I'm really sorry, Mrs Phillips,' says a very guilty Ben.

But Shawn doesn't feel sorry or guilty. Shawn feels angry at Mrs Phillips. He knows if she tells his mum what he did he won't be allowed to watch TV for a week. And he loves TV!

While Ben sits and thinks about how laughing at Shawn's picture was wrong and how he doesn't blame Mrs Phillips for wanting to speak to his mum, Shawn is getting angrier. 'How dare Mrs Phillips tell my mum!' thinks Shawn. 'It was only a joke!'

Shawn spots the maths book that he and Ben had been sharing on the table in front of them and throws it at the wall in anger.

'To the Headmaster's office now!' says Mrs Phillips.

The End!

Who or What Makes Us Angry?

QUESTION: Who made Shawn angry? Circle your answer.

Mrs Phillips   Ben   Shawn

When answering this question, most people (including many adults) would say Mrs Phillips. But the answer is Shawn! Let's look at why.

People

For example,
your parents.

Pets

For example, your dog.

Places

For example, school.

Situations

For example, losing at
a computer game.

Someone's actions

For example, your mum telling you off.

Do you remember all the above **triggers** from the last chapter, such as your mum telling you off? Well, people often think that these things **make** us angry.

But they don't.

You see it's not the person, the pet, the place, the situation or someone's actions that makes you angry. If it was, we would all feel and act in the same way in the same situations.

But we don't.

Think about Ben and Shawn for a moment.

- Both boys laughed in class.
- Both boys got told off by Mrs Phillips.
- Ben did not get angry but Shawn did.

QUESTION: Why do you think Shawn got angry but Ben didn't?

To help you answer that question, write how each child was thinking when Mrs Phillips told them off in the thought bubbles below.

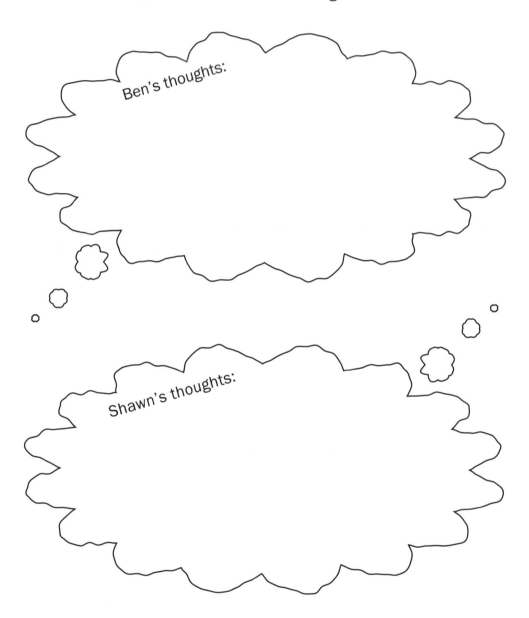

Ben's thoughts:

Shawn's thoughts:

Ben and Shawn were thinking differently from each other. This is why one got angry and the other one didn't. So what does this show us about why we get angry?

Why Do We Get Angry?

We get angry because of...

how we think!

Let's look at another example to show you what I mean by this...

Imagine that it is your school sports day. You have been really looking forward to your dad coming to watch you in the running race, but he doesn't show up.

THOUGHTS A

You might think...

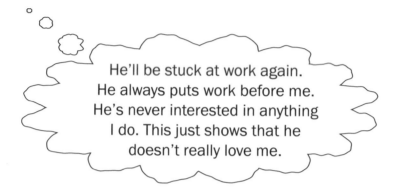

QUESTION: If you were thinking those thoughts, how angry would you be? Circle your answer.

Very angry   Angry   Not very angry

THOUGHTS B

But what if you had the following thoughts instead?

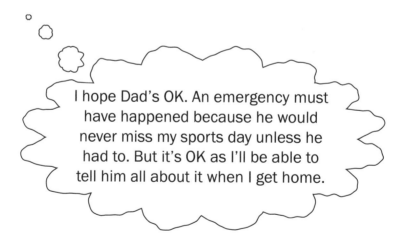

QUESTION: Now how angry do you think you would be? Circle your answer.

Very angry   Angry   Not very angry

THOUGHTS C

What if it turned out that your dad had actually broken his leg and had been at the hospital instead of at your sports day?

QUESTION: What would your thoughts be? Write them in the speech bubble below.

QUESTION: Now how angry do you think you would be? Circle your answer.

Very angry   Angry   Not very angry

I bet you would be angrier as a result of Thoughts A than Thoughts B or C! This is because Thoughts A were coming through your...

Anger Thinking Glasses!

What Are Anger Thinking Glasses?

There are two types of Anger Thinking Glasses.

Magnifying Glasses

These glasses make everything seem bigger or worse or more important than they actually are!

Make-Believe Glasses

These glasses make you imagine things to be true even though you don't know whether they are true or not!

When we get angry, we often think through our Anger Thinking Glasses. And your Anger Gremlin wants you to wear these all the time! Let's see why.

How Do Our Thoughts Feed the Anger Gremlin?

You already know that the Anger Gremlin is a troublesome pest whose favourite food is your anger, and the more anger you feed him, the bigger and bigger he gets! Well, one of the ways you feed him is by thinking thoughts through your Anger Thinking Glasses! The more you think through your Anger Thinking Glasses, the more you feed your Anger Gremlin and the bigger and bigger he gets!

And the bigger the Anger Gremlin gets, the angrier you will get.

Congratulations on completing Step 5 in starving your Anger Gremlin. Praise yourself and colour in your fifth **Starving the Anger Gremlin Star**!

Now complete one or both of the following **Just for Fun Puzzles** as a reward for all your hard work! Have fun!

Match Four!

There are lots of pictures of Gremlins on the next page. Your task is to find four identical Anger Gremlins amongst them all. Good luck!

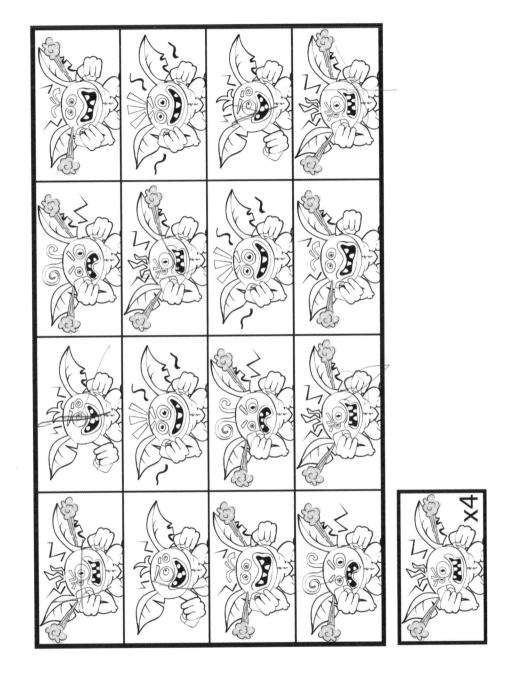

Word Jigsaw

The letter tiles below contain the following important message:

THE BIGGER YOUR ANGER GREMLIN THE ANGRIER YOU ARE.

But the Anger Gremlin has jumbled up the tiles! See if you can put them back in the correct order to spell out the message! If it makes it easier, photocopy this page and cut out the tiles and put them back together like a jigsaw. Or you can draw them in the correct order at the bottom of this page.

THE	ER Y	R GR
BIGG	ANGE	EMLI
N TH	E AN	U ARE
GRIE	OUR	R YO

7

Our Angry Bodies

Step 6 in your mission to starve your Anger Gremlin is to learn about physical feelings of anger and how they feed your Anger Gremlin.

Physical Feelings

When you get angry you will have physical feelings of anger in your body. Complete the puzzle below to learn about different types of angry physical feelings.

I Spy Scramble!

Below are pictures of different physical feelings that we can have when we get angry and labels describing them. But the Anger Gremlin has been naughty again and scrambled up the letters in each label.

1. See if you can unscramble the letters.

2. See how many physical feelings you can spy that begin with the letter 'S'.

I've unscrambled two of the labels for you to start you off.

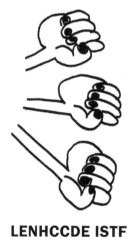

LENHCCDE ISTF

Answer: **CLENCHED FIST**

STAF BERAHTNGI

Answer: **FAST BREATHING**

KNTO NI STOACHM

Answer:

— — — — —   — —

— — — — — — —

SHKIANG

Answer:

— — — — — — —

STAF HEATR BETA

Answer:

— — — —

— — — — —

— — — —

TOH

Answer:

— — —

WEATNIGS

DER FAEC

Answer:

— — — — — — — —

Answer:

— — —   — — — —

Your Angry Body

Below are the same physical feelings pictures. Circle any that you feel when you get angry.

When I'm angry I have...

How Physical Feelings Feed Your Anger Gremlin

The more angry physical feelings you have, the more you feed your Anger Gremlin! And the bigger he continues to get! And the bigger he gets, the angrier you get.

Well done for completing Step 6 in starving your Anger Gremlin. Colour in your sixth **Starving the Anger Gremlin Star** as your reward.

Now complete one or both of the following **Just for Fun Puzzles** as a reward for being such a hard worker! Enjoy!

The Anger Gremlin Goes Line Dancing!

One of the lines below leads to the Anger Gremlin. Have a guess which one you think it is, then trace them with your finger to find out if you are correct!

Draw the Anger Gremlin!

Draw the Anger Gremlin in the grid below square by square.

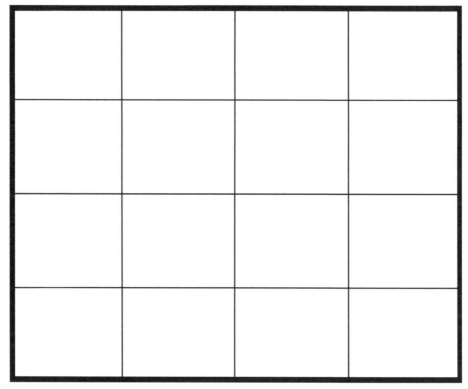

8

Our Angry Behaviours

Step 7 in your mission to starve your Anger Gremlin is to learn about angry behaviours that aren't good for you.

Angry Behaviours

When we get angry we can act in a number of different ways. Some of these behaviours can have bad effects for us or other people. Complete the puzzle below to learn about these angry behaviours.

How Good Is Your Memory?

This is a two-part puzzle. On the next page are lots of pictures of angry behaviours that aren't good for you. And in the middle of them all is a box containing words that describe those angry behaviours.

1.   Match up the words and pictures.

2.   Look at the pictures for 30 seconds. Then cover up the page and see how many angry behaviours you can remember in one minute!

Kick

Hit

Cry

Shove

Break things

Slam doors

Hurt self

Bottle anger up

Throw things

Say nasty things

Shout

Your Angry Behaviours

Below are the same negative angry behaviours pictures. Circle any that you do when you get angry.

When I'm angry I...

How Angry Behaviours Feed Your Anger Gremlin

When you act in angry ways that aren't good for you, you feed your Anger Gremlin. The more you feed him by acting in these ways a lot, the bigger he gets and the more likely it is that you will get angry more often!

How Often Do You Get Angry?

QUESTION: How often do you get angry? Circle your answer.

Most of the time   Often   Sometimes

Rarely   Never

The more often you get angry, the more you feed your Anger Gremlin and he continues to grow and grow.

The result is lots of bad effects for you and other people. We'll look at these in the next chapter. But first, congratulate yourself on completing Step 7 in starving your Anger Gremlin and colour in your seventh **Starving the Anger Gremlin Star** as your reward.

Now complete one or both of the following **Just for Fun Puzzles** as a reward for all your amazing learning so far! Enjoy!

Spot the Difference

Below are two pictures. Although they might look identical at first glance, they aren't! See if you can spot the eight differences between the two pictures. Mark the differences on the bottom picture. Have fun!

Find the Missing Letters

I have written a sentence below but the Anger Gremlin has stolen a letter from each word in the sentence! There are letters in tiles at the bottom of the page. Write the correct letter in the correct place to complete the sentence.

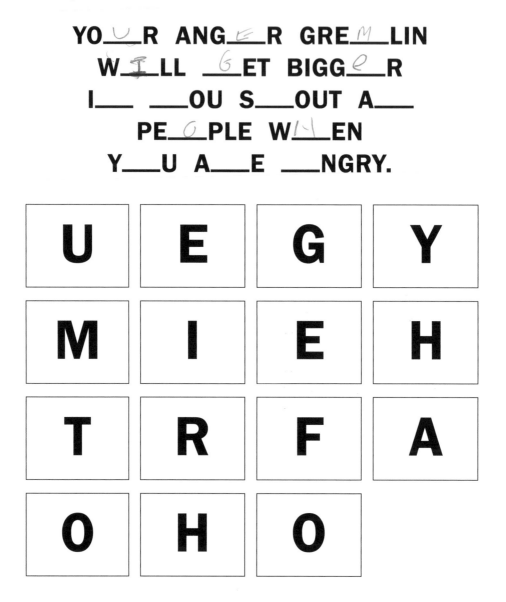

YO__R ANG_E_R GRE_M_LIN
W_I_LL _G_ET BIGG_e_R
I__ __OU S__OUT A__
PE_o_PLE W_h_EN
Y__U A__E __NGRY.

U	E	G	Y
M	I	E	H
T	R	F	A
O	H	O	

9

The Effects Anger Can Have

Step 8 in your mission to starve your Anger Gremlin is learning about the bad effects that being angry a lot can have for you and people around you. Let's look at what some of these can be through a number of activities!

What Happens Next?

Below is a story about an eight-year-old boy called Victor. But it's not finished. I would like you to read the story so far and then write or draw its ending! Make sure your ending shows the effects that Victor's anger has on him and the people around him.

The Great Football Battle!

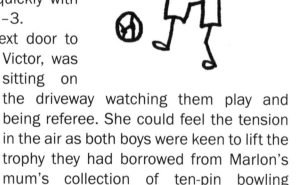

Victor and his friend Marlon were playing football in Victor's front garden. Marlon scored the first goal with a diving header. Victor scored the next one with an outstanding left-footed shot. Marlon scored two more within the next few minutes. But Victor came back quickly with two more goals. It was 3–3.

Deena, who lived next door to Victor, was sitting on

the driveway watching them play and being referee. She could feel the tension in the air as both boys were keen to lift the trophy they had borrowed from Marlon's mum's collection of ten-pin bowling trophies!

Deena watched as Victor took the lead with a stunning goal from the halfway line.

But Marlon fought back hard and in no time the score was 5–4 to Marlon!

At this crucial point in the match, Victor's mum shouted from the front door, 'Marlon, your mum rang. You need to go home for your dinner!'

Victor pleaded with Marlon to stay and play for five more minutes so that he could have a chance to score another goal and draw the match.

'Sorry, mate, but I'll get in trouble if I'm late for dinner! Better luck next time, pal!' Marlon picked up the trophy and started doing a victory lap around Victor's garden! Deena giggled. But Victor felt angry. His face went scarlet and his heart started to pound in his chest. How dare Marlon end the game just because his dinner was ready? 'It's so unfair!' Victor thought.

Victor picked up the football and kicked it towards Marlon. But Marlon ducked and the ball hit Victor's mum's car, smashing the window and sending a piece of glass into Deena's arm...

Please Continue in the Box on the Next Page!

Now answer the following questions about the story you have just read.

QUESTION: Did Victor see things through Anger Thinking Glasses? Circle your answer.

Yes   No

QUESTION: What physical feelings of anger did Victor have?

.He......was.....Triens.....to..hurt..
Marlon.

QUESTION: How did Victor act?

Victor...acted...angsily.........

QUESTION: Which of the following did Victor do? Circle your answer.

Starve his Anger Gremlin   Feed his Anger Gremlin

The Day I Got Angry

Now I'd like you to write your own story or draw a comic strip called 'The Day I Got Angry'. You can use the box on the next page or a separate piece of paper.

The Day I Got Angry

Now answer the following questions about the day you got angry.

QUESTION: Did you see things through Anger Thinking Glasses? Circle your answer.

Yes   No

QUESTION: What physical feelings of anger did you have?

. . . .

. . . .

. . . .

QUESTION: How did you act?

. . . .

. . . .

. . . .

QUESTION: Which of the following did you do? Circle your answer.

Starve your Anger Gremlin   Feed your Anger Gremlin

QUESTION: What effects did your anger have on you and other people around you?

. . . .

. . . .

. . . .

. . . .

Effects of Anger on You

If you get angry a lot it can have lots of bad effects on you. Here are some pictures showing you some of the effects that anger can have. You have probably used some of these in the two activities you have just completed. Circle or colour in the pictures that show how your anger has affected you.

**You can end up
in lots of arguments**

**You can end up
in lots of trouble**

**You can end
up lonely**

**You can end up
excluded from school**

**You can end up
with headaches or
stomach aches**

**You can end up
feeling sad, unhappy,
guilty or ashamed**

You can end up getting lower grades at school

Effects of Anger on Other People

If you get angry a lot, it can have bad effects on other people too, such as your family, friends and teachers.

Here are some pictures showing you two bad effects that anger can have on other people. You may have used both of these in the two activities you have just completed. Circle or colour in these pictures if you feel your anger has affected other people in these ways.

Other people can feel worried, stressed, upset, scared or unhappy as a result of your anger

Other people can get physically hurt as a result of your anger

So now you know the bad effects that your anger can have on you and other people around you. But here is something you may not have realised until now...the more of these bad effects that you experience, the harder it will be to stop feeling angry. So you are more likely to carry on feeding your Anger Gremlin until he gets so big he is...

MASSIVE

HUGE

ENORMOUS

and even

GINORMOUS!

And when this happens you will feel like it is impossible to stop being angry. It will feel like you have no control over your anger. But guess what? You do!

You are in control of your anger because you have the choice to feed or starve your Anger Gremlin!

Reward yourself for completing Step 8 in starving your Anger Gremlin by colouring in your eighth **Starving the Anger Gremlin Star**!

Now complete one or both of the following **Just for Fun Puzzles** as a reward for working so hard! Enjoy!

Hidden Gremlins!

There are five Anger Gremlins hidden in the picture below. See if you can spot all five! Mark the Gremlins on the picture.

Picture Suduko

Complete the picture suduko below. You need to make sure that there is one of each of the following three pictures on each horizontal and vertical row. I have started it for you.

10

Starving the Anger Gremlin Strategies

Before you can complete your mission to starve your Anger Gremlin you first need to know what he looks like!

Draw Your Own Anger Gremlin

Think about how your Anger Gremlin might look and draw him in the box below or on your own piece of paper. Then give him a name! On the next page is one that was drawn by Mollie aged six years.

My Anger Gremlin named

. . . .

**Angroman the Anger
Gremlin by Mollie
aged six years**

OK, now you know what your Anger Gremlin looks like, let's move on to Step 9 in your mission to starve him. This involves learning how to do two things...

Think differently	**Act differently**

Think Differently

Do you remember that it is how you think about a person, pet, place, situation or another person's actions that causes your anger? Do you remember that if you think through Anger Thinking Glasses you are feeding your Anger Gremlin? To stop this and to starve your Anger Gremlin you need to...

think differently!

Be a Thought Detective!

When you feel yourself getting angry, you need to try and think like a **Thought Detective** instead. This means searching for things called **facts** just like a detective searching for evidence. Facts are the things that we know are definitely true.

To search for the facts ask yourself questions such as:

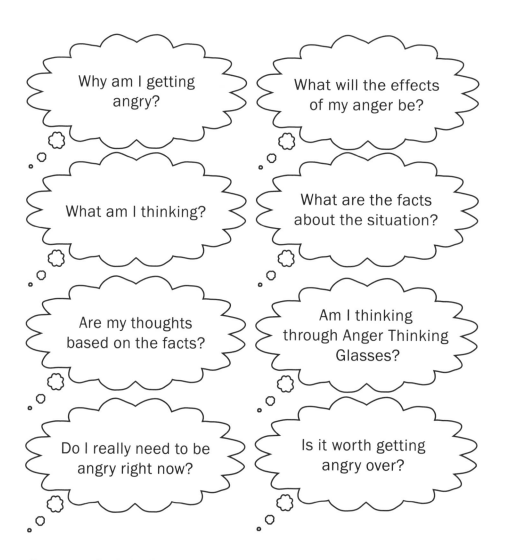

Why am I getting angry?

What will the effects of my anger be?

What am I thinking?

What are the facts about the situation?

Are my thoughts based on the facts?

Am I thinking through Anger Thinking Glasses?

Do I really need to be angry right now?

Is it worth getting angry over?

Once you find the facts you can use them to think differently!

If you become a Thought Detective and begin thinking differently by searching for the facts, the following things should start to happen:

- You should realise that sometimes you are getting angry when you don't need to.
- You should be able to calm yourself down more easily.
- You should get angry less and less.
- You should help to starve your Anger Gremlin.
- Your Anger Gremlin should start to shrink!

Let's practise being a Thought Detective and searching for the facts using the story on the next page.

The Birthday Girl Gets Angry!

It's Sophie's sixth birthday party today and she is very excited! She puts on her favourite dress and helps her mum to ice all the party cupcakes. But her mum keeps the big birthday cake hidden from Sophie so it will be a surprise!

The party starts at 2pm and, right on time, Sophie's friends arrive one by one and fill up Sophie's garden. But by 2.30pm, Sophie's best friend, Heather, hasn't arrived.

'Don't worry, sweetie pie,' says Sophie's mum when she sees the disappointed look on her daughter's face. 'Heather will be here soon, I'm sure.'

They start to eat sandwiches and cupcakes, but still Heather doesn't arrive. They start to play pass the parcel and musical chairs, but still Heather doesn't arrive. They play on the bouncy castle that Sophie's parents had hired for the party, but still Heather doesn't arrive.

At 5pm, Sophie's friends all leave. Sophie waves them all goodbye with a smile on her face, but inside she isn't smiling. Inside she is angry that her best friend did not come to her party!

The End!

SOPHIE PICTURE A

Below is a picture of an angry Sophie. Write some angry thoughts that you think Sophie might have about Heather not turning up to her party in the thought bubble.

You might have written thoughts like:

SOPHIE PICTURE B

Now we have a picture of a calm-looking Sophie because she has become a Thought Detective and has searched for the facts. Write some fact-based thoughts that Sophie could have about her best friend not coming to her party in the speech bubble.

You might have written the following fact-based thoughts or ones that are similar:

QUESTION: Which set of thoughts starve Sophie's Anger Gremlin? Circle your answer.

Thoughts in Sophie Picture A   Thoughts in Sophie Picture B

The thoughts in Picture B starve Sophie's Anger Gremlin because she is searching for the facts like a good Thought Detective. But in Picture A Sophie is thinking through her Anger Thinking Glasses and is feeding her Anger Gremlin.
So whenever you find yourself feeling angry starve your Anger Gremlin by:

- ditching your Anger Thinking Glasses!
- being a Thought Detective searching for the facts!

Now you have learnt about different ways to become a great Thought Detective and to ditch your Anger Thinking Glasses, draw a picture of yourself as a Thought Detective searching for the facts and ditching your Anger Thinking Glasses in the box on the next page!

Me as a Thought Detective!

Act Differently

Sometimes as a Thought Detective you will search for the facts and find that you have a real reason to be angry. For example if **someone says or does hurtful things to you** or if **something unfair happens**.

But even if this happens, you don't have to shout or scream or hit or break things as those things feed your Anger Gremlin! You have a choice to act differently. Here is a story to show you what I mean.

Problems in the Playground!

Seven-year-old Chris is walking through the school playground at playtime when an older boy pushes him over. The older boy walks away from Chris laughing.

At first Chris is shocked. But then Chris becomes very angry. Chris picks himself up off the ground and walks over to the older boy and hits him.

A teacher sees Chris hit the older boy and sends Chris to the Headteacher's office.

The End!

Follow the Lines to Starve Chris's Anger Gremlin

Even though Chris had a real reason to be angry, by hitting the boy he was feeding his Anger Gremlin. One of the lines in the puzzle on the next page leads to a way that Chris could have acted that would have starved his Anger Gremlin instead of feeding it. See if you can work out which line it is!

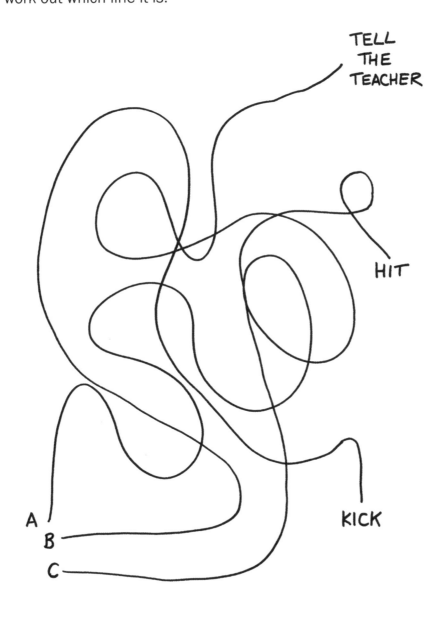

Practical Ways to Starve Your Anger Gremlin

Here are some things you can do when you feel angry for a real reason to help you deal with the situation practically instead of spending all your time feeling angry. By doing these you will be starving your Anger Gremlin!

Talk

You can talk calmly to the person you are angry with, telling them how you feel and discussing how to solve the situation you are angry about.

You can also talk to someone who you trust, like a teacher, about how you are feeling. They can help you to become a Thought Detective and search for the facts. They can also help you to work out what to do to resolve the problem that has led you to be angry.

Create an Anger Box

You can draw or write down the things that make you angry and put them in your Anger Box. Then when you feel calmer you can take them out and be a Thought Detective. If you realise there is no longer any need to be angry about those things, you can throw the pieces of paper away along with your anger! But if you find you have a real reason to be angry you will be calm enough now to work out how to solve the problem.

Why not have a go at making your own Anger Box? You can design and decorate it how you like!

Fill in an Anger Diary

Often writing or drawing about your anger can help you to be a Thought Detective and search for the facts. It can also help you to work out what you can do to resolve a problem or how you can act better next time a similar thing happens. You will find an example diary on the next page.

Anger Diary

Write or draw your answers to the following questions in the spaces below.

Date . . . .

What did you get angry about today?

```
┌─────────────────────────────────────────┐
│                                         │
│                                         │
│                                         │
│                                         │
└─────────────────────────────────────────┘
```

What were your thoughts?

```
┌─────────────────────────────────────────┐
│                                         │
│                                         │
│                                         │
│                                         │
└─────────────────────────────────────────┘
```

Did you think through Anger Thinking Glasses? Circle your answer.

Yes   No

What angry physical feelings did you have?

```
┌─────────────────────────────────────────┐
│                                         │
│                                         │
│                                         │
└─────────────────────────────────────────┘
```

How did you act?

What effects did your anger have on you and other people around you?

Which of the following did you do? Circle your answer.

Starve your Anxiety Gremlin   Feed your Anxiety Gremlin

If you fed him, what could you have done differently to starve him?

Problem solve

It is better to try and deal with a problem instead of getting angrier and angrier about it! Ask yourself three questions to help you do this:

1. What is the problem that I am angry about?

2. What things could I do about it?

3. Which one would bring the best results and starve my Anger Gremlin?

Ignore

Sometimes the best way to starve your Anger Gremlin is to ignore something that you feel angry about. Sometimes it's not worth wasting your time on doing anything else.

Be Calm

Here are some things you can do when you feel angry to help you calm down either because the facts show you that you don't need to be angry or because you need to be calm to solve a problem. All of these will help you to starve your Anger Gremlin!

Count to ten

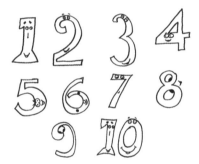

Counting to ten gives you time to calm down!

Exercise

Exercise will help you to get rid of all those angry physical feelings!

Relax

Take deep breaths and do things that make you feel chilled, such as reading a book, watching TV, listening to music or playing a game!

Visualise

This means picturing something that makes you feel calm or happy or something that makes you laugh in your head. This will help you feel calmer in no time!

Walk away

Walking away gives you time to calm down! Having a happy or calm place that you can walk away to when you feel angry helps as well.

Distract yourself

Distract yourself from feeling angry by doing things that you enjoy!

Sleep

Getting enough sleep is really important! If we are too tired because we haven't slept enough, we can be more likely to get angry about something when we don't need to.

Let's look at how some of the calming strategies might help you to starve your Anger Gremlin. You can write or draw your answers in the boxes below.

My choice of exercise would be...	**My way to relax would be...**
My way to distract myself would be...	**My happy or calm picture in my mind would be...**
My calm place to walk away to would be...	**The person I would talk to would be...**

Feed or Starve?

Below are a number of different pictures. I want you to write down underneath each one whether you think they feed or starve the Anger Gremlin.

Well done! You've completed Step 9 in starving your Anger Gremlin!
Be proud and colour in your ninth **Starving the Anger Gremlin Star**!

Now complete one or both of the following **Just for Fun Puzzles** as
a reward! Enjoy!

Missing Piece!

A jigsaw piece is missing from the picture below. See if you can work out which piece it is. Circle your answer.

Starve the Anger Gremlin Fill-In Puzzle

Below are some of the ways to starve your Anger Gremlin. See if you can complete the puzzle below by fitting all the words into the crossword grid. Each word shares at least one letter with another word in the list.

HINT: Start with the 9-letter word!

3-Letter	4-Letter	5-Letter
BOX	TALK	SLEEP
	CALM	WRITE
	WALK	RELAX
		SOLVE
		DIARY
		COUNT

6-Letter	8-Letter	9-Letter
IGNORE	EXERCISE	VISUALISE
	DISTRACT	

11

Your Anger Dos and Don'ts!

For the next two activities you'll need some paper, pens, crayons or paints and even some glue and glitter if you like!

Anger Dos and Don'ts Chart

Now it's time for you to think about everything you have learnt throughout this book and create your own Anger Dos and Don'ts Chart. Try and come up with at least five of each.

It can help to have one of these pinned up somewhere at home so you can look at it and remind yourself of what you need to do to starve your Anger Gremlin. You can even make a second one to keep in your school bag!

Have fun creating your chart and decorate it however you like. Use your imagination!

Starving the Anger Gremlin Sticker Chart

Some children find that creating a Starving the Anger Gremlin Sticker Chart can help them to see just how well they are doing at starving their Anger Gremlin. There is an example one on the next page which breaks the day down into different times. But you can design your chart in the way that works best for you. Have fun creating your chart and again you can decorate it however you like.

Once you've made your chart you need to stick on a 'Starve the Anger Gremlin Star' every time you manage to starve your Anger Gremlin. But you need to stick on an Anger Gremlin picture when you act in a way that feeds your Anger Gremlin. On page 140 there are lots of stars and Gremlins. You can photocopy this page and then cut out the stars and Gremlins for use with your chart or you can use different stickers that you might have at home if you prefer.

Monday

Getting ready for school	
Breakfast	
Journey to school	
At school	
Journey home from school	
After school	
Eating dinner	
After dinner	
Going to bed	

STICKERS

Well done! I bet your Dos and Don'ts Chart and your Sticker Chart look great! Completing one or both of these charts was Step 10 in your mission to starve your Anger Gremlin. Colour in your tenth **Starving the Anger Gremlin Star** to celebrate!

Now complete one or both of the following **Just for Fun Puzzles** as a reward for having learnt so much about how to starve your Anger Gremlin! Enjoy!

Memory Game!

- STEP A: Read through your Dos and Don'ts Chart for one minute.
- STEP B: Cover up your chart and see how many dos and don'ts you can remember in one minute!

Good luck!

Crack the Code!

Below is an important message written in code. You need to crack this code to reveal its hidden message! I've told you what some of the symbols mean but not all of them. Happy code breaking!

THE MESSAGE

1 * △ 2 □ 3

 # @ 4 2

△ 5 + 3 2

+ 2 3 ? 6 ⌂ 5 7

THE CODE

1 = S	6 = ___	# = Y
2 = R	7 = !	+ = G
3 = ___	△ = A	* = ___
4 = ___	? = M	□ = ___
5 = ___	⌂ = I	@ = ___

12

Completing Your Mission to Starve the Anger Gremlin!

Congratulations! You have now learnt all you need to know about anger and how to starve your Anger Gremlin. It's now down to you to put it into practice. This is the final step in your mission to starve your Anger Gremlin. Remember...

You are in control of your anger!

You can choose to starve your Anger Gremlin!

Here is a quiz to help you recap on everything you have learnt throughout this workbook.

The Anger Quiz

1. **Fill in the blank. Another word for a feeling is an**

    E __ __ __ __ __

2. **Colour in the odd one out. HINT: The odd one out is not a feeling!**

3. **Name two feelings beginning with the letter 'S'. HINT: Take a look at these two faces!**

. . . .

4. **Unscramble the word. Anger is a GLEFENI.**

   F __ __ __ __ __ __

5. **Everyone feels angry at times. Circle the correct answer.**

   True   False

6. **Anger can become a problem. Circle the correct answer.**

   True   False

7. **Unscramble these anger triggers.**

   a. LACPES   P __ __ __ __ __

   b. PEEPLO   P __ __ __ __ __

   c. TEPS   P __ __ __

   d. SITNUAIOTS   S __ __ __ __ __ __ __ __

8. **Which of these are negative angry behaviours? Tick your answers.**

   a. Hit ☐

   b. Kick ☐

   c. Relax ☐

   d. Problem solve ☐

9. **Which of these are physical feelings of anger? Tick your answers.**

   a. Sweating ☐

   b. Shaking ☐

   c. Red face ☐

   d. Blowing your nose ☐

10. Who is in control of your anger? Tick the correct answer.

a. You ☐

b. Your parents ☐

c. Your dog ☐

d. The Anger Gremlin ☐

11. What do you need to do to the Anger Gremlin? Tick the correct answer.

a. Starve it ☐

b. Feed it ☐

c. Hug it ☐

12. Which of these are ways to starve the Anger Gremlin? Tick your answers.

a. Talk ☐

b. Distract yourself ☐

c. Walk away ☐

d. Shout ☐

e. Break things ☐

Has Your Anger Changed?

Here are some questions to help you see if your anger has changed in any way as you have worked through this book. I've asked you most of these questions before earlier in this workbook. I have introduced three new questions as well.

QUESTION 1

How often do you get angry? Circle your answer.

Most of the time   Often   Sometimes

Rarely   Never

QUESTION 2

Below are some negative angry behaviours pictures. Circle any that you do when you get angry.

QUESTION 3

Here are some pictures of the different bad effects that anger can have. Circle or colour in the pictures that show how your anger is still affecting you.

 Lots of arguments

In lots of trouble

 Headaches or stomach aches

Excluded from school

Feeling sad, unhappy, guilty or ashamed

Being lonely

 Getting lower grades at school

QUESTION 4

Do you now do any of the following to starve your Anger Gremlin?

Talk

Use an Anger Box

Fill in an Anger Diary

Problem solve

Ignore

Walk away

Count to ten

Exercise

Relax

Distract yourself

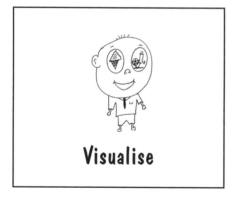

Visualise

Sleep

QUESTION 5

Colour in your answer. Since starting this book...

I haven't starved my Anger Gremlin at all	**I have starved my Anger Gremlin a little**	**I have starved my Anger Gremlin a lot**

QUESTION 6

Colour in your answer. Since starting this book my anger has...

Got less	**Stayed the same**	**Got worse**

What You Have Learnt

Now let's look at what you feel you have learnt by completing this workbook. Tick the box for each item that you feel you have learnt.

I understand that anger is a feeling. ☐

I understand that it is normal to get angry sometimes. ☐

I understand that if I feed my Anger Gremlin too often my anger will become a problem. ☐

I can name some angry physical feelings. ☐

I can name some negative ways that people might act when they get angry. ☐

I can name different types of anger triggers. ☐

I am aware of some of my own anger triggers. ☐

I understand that it's how I think about a situation that leads me to be angry not the situation itself. ☐

I understand what feeds my Anger Gremlin. ☐

I understand the types of thoughts that feed my Anger Gremlin. ☐

I understand the types of behaviours that feed my Anger Gremlin. ☐

I understand that feeding my Anger Gremlin too often can have bad effects on me and I can name some of these effects. ☐

I understand that feeding my Anger Gremlin can have a bad effect on other people and I can name some of these effects. ☐

I understand that I am in control of my anger. ☐

I understand that I can choose to starve my Anger Gremlin. ☐

I am aware of different ways to starve my Anger Gremlin. ☐

I hope you have found that you have learnt lots and that your anger has started to improve. Here is your final **Starving the Anger Gremlin Star** as a reward for everything you have learnt and achieved. Congratulations! You should be so proud of yourself! Have fun colouring in your star and remember you can keep collecting these stars as you work on starving your Anger Gremlin!

And here is your final **Just for Fun Puzzle** as a final reward! Enjoy!

The Anger Gremlin Fact-File!

This fact-file contains all the facts that you have learnt about the Anger Gremlin. But some of the words are missing. Try and fill in the blanks! And then colour in your final Anger Gremlin picture!

The Anger G __ __ __ __ __ __ is a troublesome pest.

The Anger Gremlin loves it when you get A __ __ __ __

If you think through Anger Thinking Glasses, you F __ __ __ the Anger Gremlin.

Angry physical F __ __ __ __ __ __ __ feed the Anger Gremlin.

Angry behaviours that are bad for you feed the A __ __ __ __ Gremlin.

The more you F __ __ __ the Anger Gremlin, the bigger he gets.

The B __ __ __ __ __ the Anger Gremlin gets, the angrier you get.

The angrier you get, the more bad effects your A __ __ __ __ has on you and other people.

And the A __ __ __ __ Gremlin gets even bigger!

But if you think differently and A __ __ differently, you can starve the Anger Gremlin.

If you are a T __ __ __ __ __ __ Detective, you starve the Anger Gremlin.

If you act in practical and calm ways, you S __ __ __ __ __ the Anger Gremlin.

If you S __ __ __ __ __ the Anger Gremlin, he will get smaller and smaller and you will get less and less angry!

Good luck with starving your Anger Gremlin!

You can do it!

This is to certify that

· ·

has successfully completed the
Starving the Anger Gremlin
workbook and can expertly

STARVE THEIR ANGER
GREMLIN!

Activity, Puzzle and Quiz Answers

Escape the Anger Gremlin!

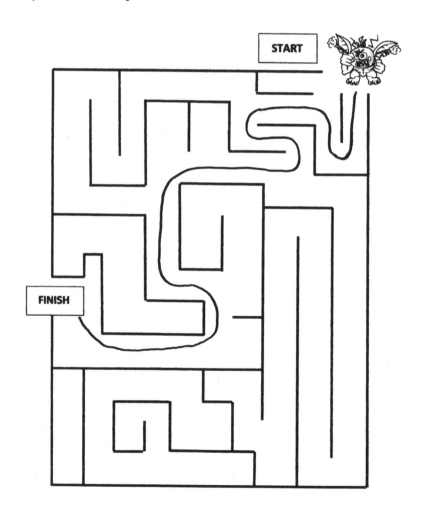

Gremlins Galore!

There are 22 Anger Gremlins in the triangle.

Word Multiplication!

Some of the words you might have spotted include germ, green, the, anger, gremlin, linger, green, men, rant, hat, heat, line...and the list goes on and on!

Feelings or Not Feelings? You Decide!

The feelings are guilty, nervous, calm, relaxed, surprised, jealous, afraid and upset.

Find the Feelings!

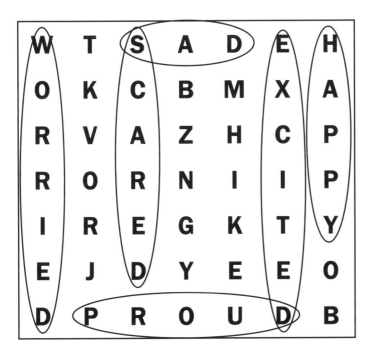

The Face and Feeling Mix-Up!

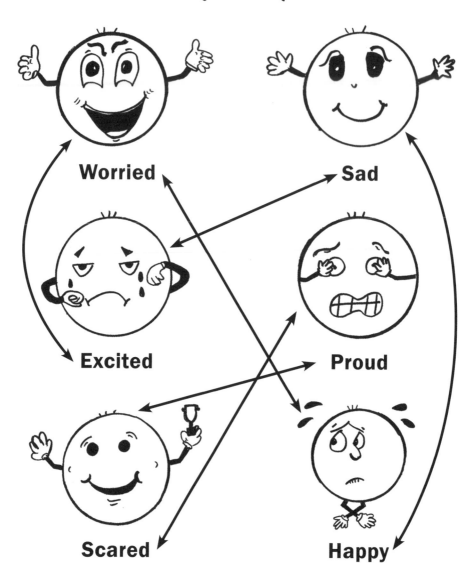

Worried

Sad

Excited

Proud

Scared

Happy

'What Am I?' Riddle

The answer is 'Feelings'.

Different Words for Angry

The words are mad, cross, annoyed and furious.

Find the Pairs!

Sammie is Reason 1

Pippa is Reason 4

Karl is Reason 5

Thomas is Reason 3

Jenny is Reason 6

Mollie is Reason 2

Go Dotty!

The picture reveals the Anger Gremlin!

Word Hunt

The word 'anger' appears seven times.

Angry Amy's Awfully Angry Day!

The pictures go into the story in the following order: parents, cat, rabbit, goldfish, grandparents. The elephant is not used!

How Many Gremlins?

There are 18 Anger Gremlins in this chapter.

Odd Gremlin Out

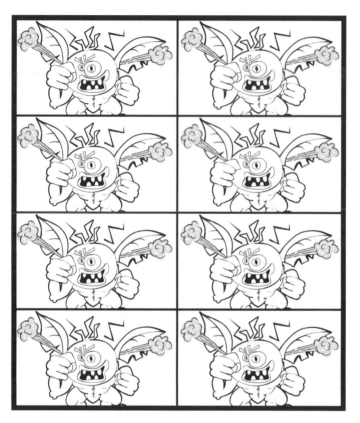

This is the odd Gremlin out.

Match Four!

The four matching Gremlins are marked with an X.

Word Jigsaw

T H E	**B I G G**	**E R Y**	**O U R**
A N G E	**R G R**	**E M L I**	**N T H**
E A N	**G R I E**	**R Y O**	**U A R E**

I Spy Scramble!

The pictures are: clenched fist, fast breathing, knot in stomach, shaking, fast heart beat, hot, sweating, red face.

There are two physical feelings beginning with the letter 'S'.

The Anger Gremlin Goes Line Dancing!

The answer is B.

How Good Is Your Memory?

Spot the Difference

The differences are marked with an X.

Find the Missing Letters

The sentence is:

Your Anger Gremlin will get bigger if you shout at people when you are angry.

Hidden Gremlins!

The Gremlins are marked with an X.

Picture Suduko

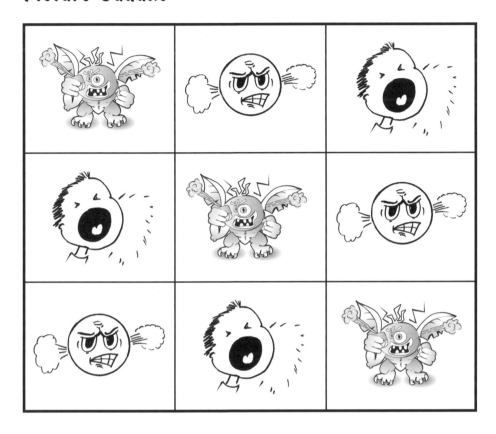

Follow the Lines to Starve
Chris's Anger Gremlin

The answer is Line A.

Feed or Starve?

Missing Piece!

The missing piece is A.

Starve the Anger Gremlin Fill-In Puzzle

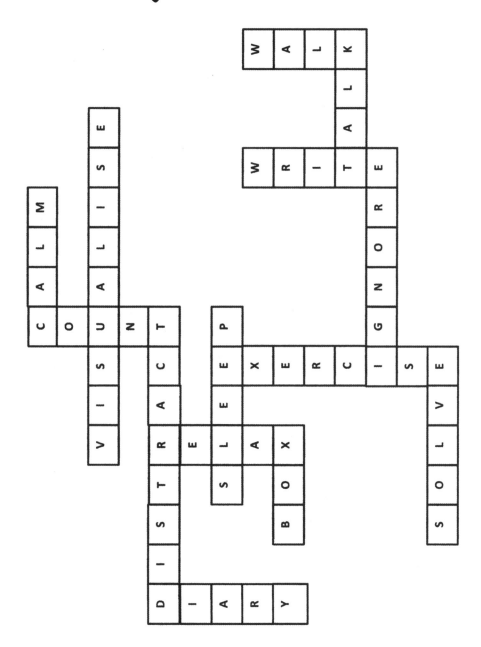

Crack the Code!

The message is: STARVE YOUR ANGER GREMLIN.
Here is the completed code grid:

1 = S	**6 = L**	**# = Y**
2 = R	**7 = !**	**+ = G**
3 = E	**△ = A**	*** = T**
4 = U	**? = M**	**□ = V**
5 = N	**⌂ = I**	**@ = O**

The Anger Quiz

1.   Emotion

2.   The odd one out is yawn as it is not a feeling

3.   You could have put scared or surprised or sad

4.   Feeling

5.   True

6.   True

7.   a. Places   b. People   c. Pets   d. Situations

8.   a and b

9.   a, b and c

10. a

11. a

12. a, b and c

The Anger Gremlin Fact-File

The Anger **GREMLIN** is a troublesome pest.

The Anger Gremlin loves it when you get **ANGRY**.

If you think through Anger Thinking Glasses, you **FEED** the Anger Gremlin.

Angry physical **FEELINGS** feed the Anger Gremlin.

Angry behaviours that are bad for you feed the **ANGER** Gremlin.

The more you **FEED** the Anger Gremlin, the bigger he gets.

The **BIGGER** the Anger Gremlin gets, the angrier you get.

The angrier you get, the more bad effects your **ANGER** has on you and other people.

And the **ANGER** Gremlin gets even bigger!

But if you think differently and **ACT** differently, you can starve the Anger Gremlin.

If you are a **THOUGHT** Detective, you starve the Anger Gremlin.

If you act in practical and calm ways, you **STARVE** the Anger Gremlin.

If you **STARVE** the Anger Gremlin, he will get smaller and smaller and you will get less and less angry!

Information for Parents and Professionals

The Purpose of This Workbook

Starving the Anger Gremlin for Children Aged 5–9 provides a cognitive behavioural approach to anger management for children aged 5 to 9 years. The cognitive behavioural approach of this workbook is combined with the approach of a traditional colouring and puzzle book to create an educational yet fun resource. And as children progress through this workbook they can gain fun rewards in the form of **Starving the Anger Gremlin Stars** and **Just for Fun Puzzles** as a celebration of their learning and progress.

Starving the Anger Gremlin for Children Aged 5–9 is designed for children to work through with the support of a parent or professional, such as a mental health practitioner, teacher, mentor, teaching assistant, social worker or youth worker. The self-help materials included in this workbook are based on the principles of cognitive behavioural therapy (CBT) but do not constitute a session-by-session therapeutic programme. However, the materials contained in this workbook can be used as a resource for therapists working with children.

An evaluation checklist and a questionnaire are included in the final chapter of the workbook to enable the child to identify just how much they have learnt and how they have progressed. However, please note that neither are designed to be used as a clinical diagnostic tool.

Please note that this workbook should not be considered a substitute for professional treatment where required.

What Is Cognitive Behavioural Therapy?

CBT is an evidence-based, skills-based, structured form of psychotherapy, which emerged from Beck's Cognitive Therapy (e.g. Beck 1976) and Ellis' Rational-Emotive Therapy (e.g. Ellis 1962), as well as from the work of behaviourists such as Pavlov (e.g. Pavlov 1927) and Skinner (e.g. Skinner 1938) on classical and operant conditioning, respectively. CBT looks at the relationships between our thoughts (cognition), our feelings (emotions) and our actions (behaviours). It is based on the premise that how we interpret experiences and situations has a profound effect on our behaviours and emotions.

CBT focuses on:

- the problems that the client is experiencing in the here and now
- why the problems are occurring
- what strategies the client can use in order to address the problems.

In doing so, the CBT process empowers the client to identify:

- negative, unhealthy and unrealistic patterns of thoughts, perspectives and beliefs
- maladaptive and unhealthy patterns of behaviour
- the links between the problems the client is facing and his or her patterns of thoughts and behaviours
- how to challenge the existing patterns of thoughts and behaviours and implement alternative thoughts and behaviours that are constructive, healthy and realistic in order to address problems, manage emotions and improve wellbeing.

Thus the underlying ethos of CBT is that by addressing unhelpful patterns of thoughts and behaviours, people can change how they feel, how they view themselves, how they interact with others and how they approach life in general – thereby moving from an unhealthy cycle of reactions to a healthy one.

A wide range of empirical studies show CBT to be effective with many mental health disorders, including:

- anxiety (e.g. Cartwright-Hatton *et al.* 2004; James, Soler and Weatherall 2005)
- obsessive compulsive disorder (OCD) (e.g. O'Kearney *et al.* 2006)
- depression (e.g. Klein, Jacobs and Reinecke 2007).

Furthermore, guidelines published by the National Institute for Health and Care Excellence (NICE) recommend the use of CBT for a number of mental health issues, including depression (NICE 2005a) and OCD (NICE 2005b).

Although CBT is widely used in clinical practice with anger and although CBT-based self-help materials are available for anger sufferers to work through, empirical research studies into the effectiveness of CBT for anger are still limited. But where these studies do occur, meta-analysis is showing promising results for CBT's effectiveness with anger (e.g. Beck and Fernandez 1998; Hofman *et al.* 2012).

EFFECTIVENESS OF CBT FOR CHILDREN AND YOUNG PEOPLE

Although there has been less research conducted on the use of CBT with children and young people than there has been with adults, evidence for its effectiveness is continuing to grow and being reported in a number of reviews, such as Kazdin and Weisz (1998) and Rapee *et al.* (2000). Extensive research is still required on CBT and anger in children and young people. But where studies are available, meta-analysis is showing promising results (e.g. Sukhodolsky, Kassinove and Gorman 2004). In addition, randomised clinical trials have shown CBT to be effective with children and young people for:

- obsessive compulsive disorder (Barrett, Healy-Farrell and March 2004)
- depression (Lewinsohn and Clarke 1999)
- generalised anxiety disorder (Kendall *et al.* 1997, 2004)
- specific phobias (Silverman *et al.* 1999)
- social phobia (Spence, Donovan and Brechman-Toussaint 2000)
- school refusal (King *et al.* 1998).

References

Barrett, P., Healy-Farrell, L. and March, J.S. (2004) 'Cognitive-behavioural family treatment of childhood obsessive compulsive disorder: a controlled trial.' *Journal of the American Academy of Child and Adolescent Psychiatry 43*, 1, 46–62.

Beck, A.T. (1976) *Cognitive Therapy and Emotional Disorders*. New York: International Universities Press.

Beck, R. and Fernandez, E. (1998) 'Cognitive-Behavioral Therapy in the Treatment of Anger: A Meta-Analysis.' *Cognitive Therapy and Research 22*, 1, 63–74.

Cartwright-Hatton, S., Roberts, C., Chitsabesan, P., Fothergill, C. *et al.* (2004) 'Systematic review of the efficacy of cognitive behaviour therapies for childhood and adolescent anxiety disorders.' *British Journal of Clinical Psychology 43*, 421–436.

Ellis, A. (1962) *Reason and Emotion in Psychotherapy*. New York: Lyle-Stuart.

Hofmann, S.G., Asnaani, A., Vonk, I.J.J., Sawyer, A.T. and Fang, A. (2012) 'The Efficacy of Cognitive Behavioral Therapy: A Review of Meta-analyses.' *Cognitive Therapy and Research 36*, 5, 427–440.

James, A.A.C.J., Soler, A. and Weatherall, R.R.W. (2005) 'Cognitive behavioural therapy for anxiety disorders in children and adolescents.' *Cochrane Database of Systematic Reviews 2005*, 4 CD004690. DOI: 10.1002/14651858.CD004690.pub2.

Kazdin, A.E. and Weisz, J.R. (1998) 'Identifying and developing empirically supported child and adolescent treatments.' *Journal of Consulting and Clinical Psychology 66*, 19–36.

Kendall, P.C., Flannery-Schroeder, E., Panichelli-Mindel, S.M., Sotham-Gerow, M., Henin, A. and Warman, M. (1997) 'Therapy with youths with anxiety disorders: a second randomized clinical trial.' *Journal of Consulting and Clinical Psychology 18*, 255–270.

Kendall, P.C., Safford, S., Flannery-Schroeder, E. and Webb, A. (2004) 'Child anxiety treatment: outcomes in adolescence and impact on substance abuse and depression at 7.4 year follow-up.' *Journal of Consulting and Clinical Psychology 72*, 276–287.

King, N.J., Molloy, G.N., Heyme, D., Murphy, G.C. and Ollendick, T. (1998) 'Emotive imagery treatment for childhood phobias: a credible and empirically validated intervention?' *Behavioural and Cognitive Psychotherapy 26*, 103–113.

Klein, J.B., Jacobs, R.H. and Reinecke, M.A. (2007) 'A meta-analysis of CBT in adolescents with depression.' *Journal of the American Academy of Child and Adolescent Psychiatry 46*, 1403–1413.

Lewinsohn, P.M. and Clarke, G.N. (1999) 'Psychosocial treatments for adolescent depression.' *Clinical Psychology Review 19*, 329–342.

National Institute for Health and Care Excellence (NICE) (2005a) 'Depression in Children and Young People. Identification and Management in Primary, Community and Secondary Care.' *Clinical Guideline* 28. Available at www.nice.org.uk/guidance/CG28, accessed on 2 May 2014.

National Institute for Health and Care Excellence (NICE) (2005b) 'Obsessive Compulsive Disorder: Core Interventions in the Treatment of Obsessive Compulsive Disorder and Body Dysmorphic Disorder.' *Clinical Guideline* 31. Available at www.nice.org.uk/nicemedia/pdf/CG031niceguideline.pdf, accessed on 2 May 2014.

O'Kearney, R.T., Anstey, K., von Sanden, C. and Hunt, A. (2006) 'Behavioural and cognitive behavioural therapy for obsessive compulsive disorder in children and adolescents.' *Cochrane Database of Systematic Reviews 2006*, 4 CD004856. DOI: 10.1002/14651858.CD004856.pub2.

Pavlov, I.P. (1927) *Conditioned Reflexes: An Investigation of the Physiological Activity of the Cerebral Cortex.* Translated and edited by G.V. Anrep. London: Oxford University Press.

Rapee, R.M., Wignall, A., Hudson, J.L. and Schniering, C.A. (2000) *Treating Anxious Children and Adolescents: An Evidence-Based Approach.* Oakland, CA: New Harbinger Publications.

Silverman, W.K. Kurtines, W.M., Ginsburg, G.S., Weems, C.F., Rabian, B. and Setafini, L.T. (1999) 'Contingency management, self-control and education support in the treatment of childhood phobic disorders: a randomized clinical trial.' *Journal of Consulting and Clinical Psychology 67*, 675–687.

Skinner, B.F. (1938) *The Behavior of Organisms.* New York: Appleton-Century-Crofts.

Spence, S., Donovan, C. and Brechman-Toussaint, M. (2000) 'The treatment of childhood social phobia: the effectiveness of a social skills training-based cognitive behavioural intervention with and without parental involvement.' *Journal of Child Psychology and Psychiatry 41*, 713–726.

Sukhodolsky, D.G., Kassinove, H. and Gorman, B.S. (2004) 'Cognitive-behavioral therapy for anger in children and adolescents: a meta-analysis.' *Aggression and Violent Behavior 9*, 3, 247–269.